READY, SET, DRAW!

CATS YOU CAN DRAW

Nicole Brecke

Patricia M. Stockland

M Millbrook Press / Minneapolis

The images in this book are used with the permission of: © iStockphoto.com/Dzianis Miraniuk, p. 4;
© iStockphoto.com, pp. 4, 5; © iStockphoto.com/Boris Yankov, p. 5; © iStockphoto.com/JR Trice, p. 5;
© iStockphoto.com/Dan Moore, pp. 7, 14-15; © iStockphoto.com/Carl Kelliher, p. 9; © iStockphoto.com/
Diane Diederich, p. 11; © iStockphoto.com/Huchen Lu, pp. 18-19; © iStockphoto.com/Jennifer Sheets,
pp. 22-23; © Kavita/Fotolia.com, pp. 26-27; © iStockphoto.com/Ewa Brozek, pp. 30-31.

Front cover: © iStockphoto.com/Carl Kelliher (pillows); © iStockphoto.com/Jennifer Sheets (scratching
post); © Ron Chapple Studios/Dreamstime.com (hand).

Edited by Mari Kesselring
Research by Emily Temple

Text and illustrations copyright © 2010 by Lerner Publishing Group, Inc.

Millbrook Press
A division of Lerner Publishing Group, Inc.
241 First Avenue North
Minneapolis, MN 55401 U.S.A.

Website address: www.lernerbooks.com

Library of Congress Cataloging-in-Publication Data

Brecke, Nicole.
    Cats you can draw / by Nicole Brecke and Patricia M. Stockland ; illustrations by Nicole Brecke.
        p.   cm. — (Ready, set, draw!)
    Includes index.
    ISBN: 978–0–7613–4161–1 (lib. bdg. : alk. paper)
    1. Cats in art—Juvenile literature. 2. Drawing—Technique—Juvenile literature.
I. Stockland, Patricia M. II. Title.
NC783.8.C36B74 2010
704.9'432—dc22   2008052182

Manufactured in the United States of America
1 2 3 4 5 6 – BP – 15 14 13 12 11 10

TABLE OF CONTENTS

ABOUT THIS BOOK

Cats are graceful creatures. And drawing them is fun! With the help of this book, you can start sketching your favorites. Draw a giant Maine coon. Or color a smart, sneaky Siamese. Soon, you'll know how to draw many different cats.

Follow these steps to create each cat. Each drawing begins with a basic form. The form is made up of a line and a shape or two. These lines and shapes will help you make your drawing the correct size.

A First, read all the steps and look at the pictures. Then use a pencil to lightly draw the line and shapes shown in RED. You will erase these lines later.

B Next, draw the lines shown in BLUE.

C Keep going! Once you have completed a step, the color of the line changes to BLACK. Follow the BLUE line until you're done.

WHAT YOU WILL NEED

PENCIL SHARPENER

COLORED PENCILS

HELPFUL HINTS

Be creative. Follow your imagination. Read about your favorite cat, and then follow the steps to create your own litter of kitties!

Practice drawing different lines and shapes. All of your drawings will start with these.

Use very light pencil lines when you are drawing.

Helpful tips and hints will offer you good ideas on making the most of your sketch.

Colors are exciting. Try to use a variety of shades. This will add value, or depth, to your finished drawings.

Keep practicing, and have fun!

ERASER

PENCIL

PAPER

HOW TO DRAW A MAINE COON

The Maine coon is a long-haired breed. But not all of its hair is long. The hair on its face and paws is much shorter than the rest of its fur. This cat first became popular in Maine and other New England states. This big breed likes to be outdoors. A male Maine coon can weigh 18 pounds (8 kilograms). That's a lot bigger than other cats. Its big size and extra fur make the Maine coon a perfect cold-weather cat. These gentle and friendly cats can be striped, spotted, solid, shaded, or bicolored (two different colors).

1 Lightly draw a small oval and a curved line. Add a larger oval.

2 Draw the neck to connect the ovals. Add two pointy, tipped ears with small triangles on the top. Draw the backbone.

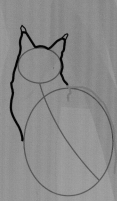

3 Use two longer bumpy lines to draw a large tail. Add two diagonal lines for the front leg. Carefully erase your base shapes and center line.

4 Draw two small ovals for eyes. Add a dark circle to the middle of each. Draw a curved line around each eye. Draw a small triangle for the nose. Connect the nose and curved lines with U shapes. Add whiskers.

5 Now it's time to color your Maine coon!

HOW TO DRAW A
RAGDOLL

Ragdoll cats are great family pets. They become relaxed and limp, just like a doll, when they are with their owners! This laid-back breed is likely a cross between Persians and Birmans. Ragdolls make patient pets. But they can be big. Some males weigh more than 20 pounds (9 kg). Ragdoll cats can be colorpoint (marked with dark fur), mitted (marked with white paws), or bicolored. Their coats have thick, medium-length fur.

1 Draw a base oval. Add a curved center line. Draw a smaller circle at one end.

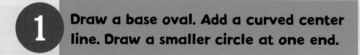

2

Draw a wide neck and head with two triangle bumps for ears. Draw the backbone and a long, curved tail.

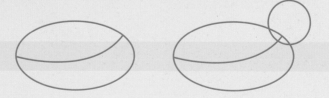

3

Draw the back hip, leg, and belly. Draw the front leg and paw. Add the other two legs.

4 Carefully erase your center line and base shapes.

5

Draw pointed ovals and circles for the eyes. Draw a small triangle for the nose. Add two mouth lines. Connect them with a curved line. Use larger curved lines for the face.

6 Now it's time to color your ragdoll!

HOW TO DRAW A PERSIAN

Do you love long-haired cats? Then a pretty, purring Persian is the perfect pick. These quiet, friendly cats have thick, silky fur. They also have short tails that are extremely fluffy. The hair on their tails can grow to 6 inches (15 centimeters) long. Persians have large, round eyes and small, rounded ears. These cats grow to between 7 and 12 pounds (3 and 5 kg). They come in more than sixty different color combinations!

1

Draw an oval with a curved center line. Add a circle to one end.

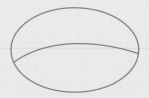 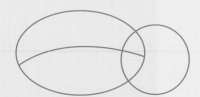

2

Draw a bumpy curved line for the backbone. Add a rough, open circle for the head. Draw two small bumps for ears.

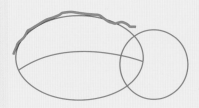 

3

Draw a large, curved tail. Add the belly line and two small ovals for the front paws. Make a small vertical line to finish the front shoulder.

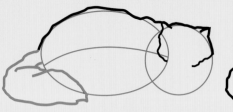

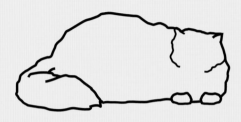

4

Carefully erase your base shapes and center line.

5

Draw two almond-shaped eyes. Add a circle and a dark oval to the middle of each. Draw a rough triangle for the face and a small triangle inside that for the nose. Add a small triangle to the tip of the larger one. Add two mouth lines.

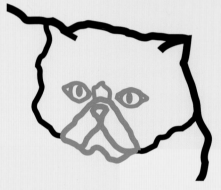

6 Now it's time to color your Persian!

HOW TO DRAW A BIRMAN

Birman cats have been compared to puppies.
That's how friendly this breed is! Birmans are also known
for their white paws. It looks as if these cats are wearing
mittens. This popular breed can have one of many different
pointed color patterns. These colorful cats also have
striking blue eyes. Legend surrounds the Birman. It's said
this breed protected priests (religious leaders) in the country
of Myanmar. Because of this, Birman cats were considered
sacred, or holy. Nowadays, these affectionate cats are
popular with families.

1 Draw a small base circle and a curved center
line. Add a large base oval.

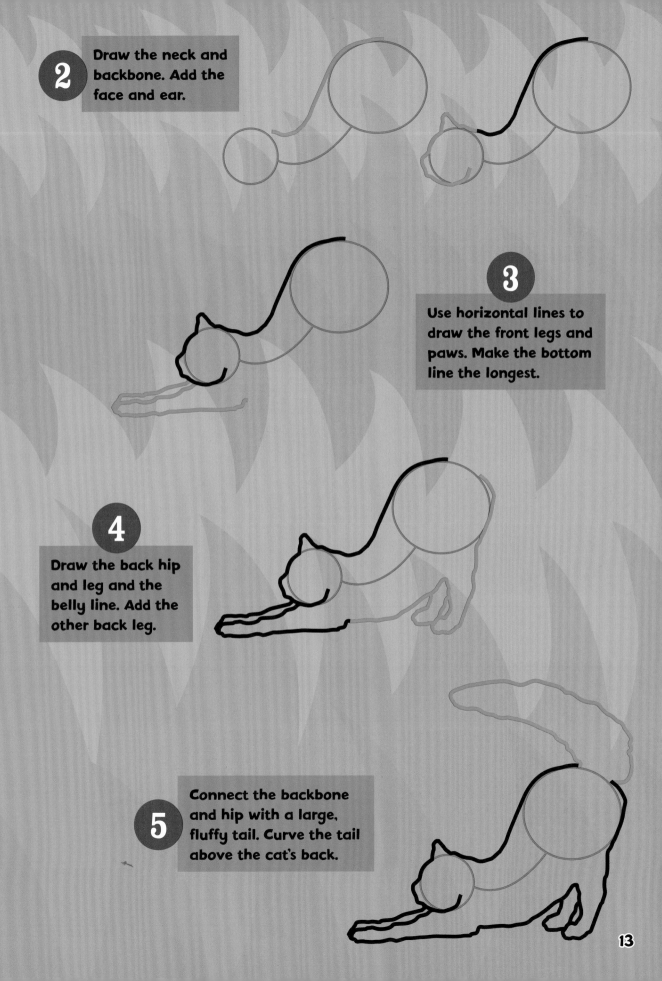

2 Draw the neck and backbone. Add the face and ear.

3 Use horizontal lines to draw the front legs and paws. Make the bottom line the longest.

4 Draw the back hip and leg and the belly line. Add the other back leg.

5 Connect the backbone and hip with a large, fluffy tail. Curve the tail above the cat's back.

13

6 Carefully erase your base shapes and center line.

7 Draw a larger eye and a small nose. Add an ear line and a small line for the back of the head.

CHECK IT OUT

Don't forget to feed your cat. A favorite food dish is a must.

DRAW A CAT DISH!

A

B

C

Stretching
helps cats
stay in great
shape.

8 Now it's time to
color your Birman!

HOW TO DRAW A SPHYNX

Want an eye-catching cat? How about a sphynx? These long, angular cats have hardly any hair! With large heads and no whiskers, sphynx cats cause quite a stir. These cats have a light, downy coat that you can barely see. The coat is usually black and white or brown and white. Sphynx cats are friendly and loving, making them good family pets. They live to be about fifteen years old. And they can weigh up to 10 pounds (4.5 kg). These cats are also very lively. Some owners compare their sphynx cats to monkeys! Sphynx cats are affectionate—be sure to give yours enough attention.

1 Draw a light base circle and a center line. Add two triangles and an oval. Draw a small head and two large ears.

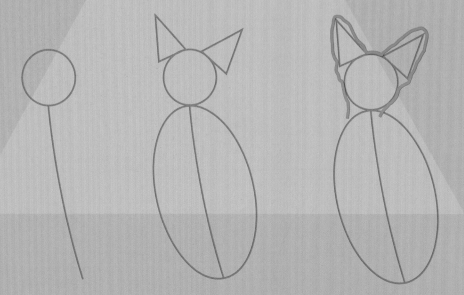

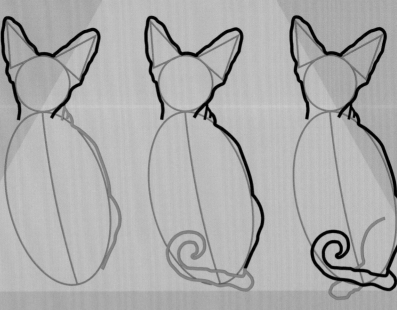

2

Draw a bumpy line to make the backbone and hip. Add a skinny, curved tail. Draw the back leg and paw.

3

Draw vertical lines for the front leg and paw. Draw the second back paw behind the front paw. Add two bent lines for the other front leg.

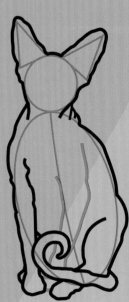

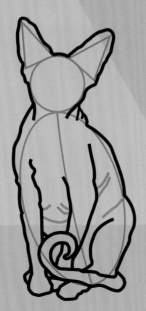

4

Add small horizontal lines to the side and stomach. These show skin wrinkles.

5 Before finishing the face, carefully erase your base shapes and center line.

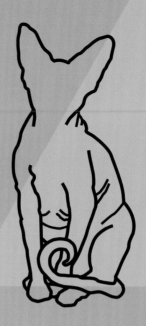

6 Draw a small triangle and two curved lines for the nose. Draw a fan shape for the mouth and jaw. Add two almond-shaped eyes. Draw a dark circle in each.

Did you know...
SOME PEOPLE WITH ALLERGIES CAN LIVE WITH SPHYNX CATS.

7 Now it's time to color your sphynx!

Sphynx cats love to show off for their owners!

QUICK TIP
Color with short, light strokes to show short, light hair.

HOW TO DRAW AN
AMERICAN SHORTHAIR

American shorthairs are hardworking cats. This sturdy breed came to North America with the early European explorers. The British used these cats to get rid of mice and rats on their ships. American shorthair cats are excellent mousers. They have compact bodies, short faces, and thick, hardy coats. They weigh from 8 to 15 pounds (3.6 to 6.8 kg) and can live more than fifteen years. American shorthair cats come in more than fifty different colors and patterns, including solid, tabby (stripes, spots, or blotches), and smoke.

1

Lightly draw a small base circle and a long center line. Add a long oval.

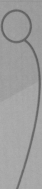

2 Draw the face and two pointy ears.

3 Draw a curved line for the neck and back. Add a long, curved tail.

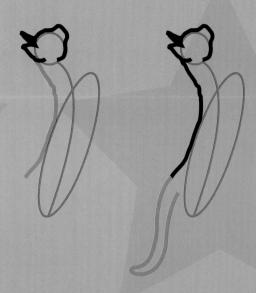

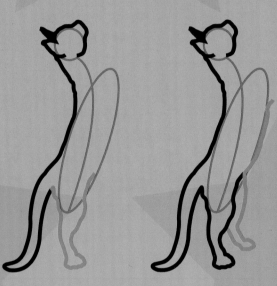

4 Add the back leg and paw. Draw the other back leg and the belly.

5 From the chest area, draw a curved front leg and paw. Add the other front leg and paw.

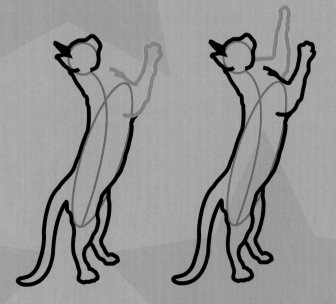

6 Carefully erase your base shapes and center line.

7 Draw a curved shape for the inside of the ear. Add a smaller round eye. Draw a small U shape for the nose.

TIME TO PLAY

Cats like to pounce and romp. Keep your cat entertained with a toy.

DRAW A CAT TOY!

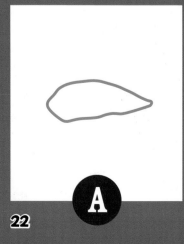

A

B

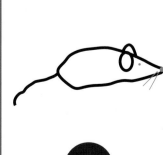

C

8 Now it's time to color your American shorthair!

TIP
Color lines in the direction the hair grows.

CATS scratch posts to keep their claws sharp.

HOW TO DRAW AN
ABYSSINIAN

Abyssinians have been around for a long time. They are one of the oldest tame cat breeds. The breed was brought to Great Britain from Ethiopia during the 1800s. Abyssinians can be a little shy. These intelligent cats like their freedom. And they don't like small spaces. This breed can be many different colors, including lavender (light gray), chocolate, and blue (dark gray to black). An Abyssinian's soft, silky coat has multiple color bands. Abyssinians can live to be more than fifteen years old.

1

Draw a base circle and a curved center line. Add an oval.

2 Draw the backbone, a long, upright tail, and the back hip.

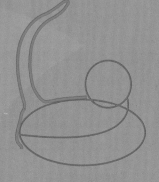

3 Draw a curved back leg and paw and a short belly line. Add the other back leg. Use vertical lines to draw the front legs and chest.

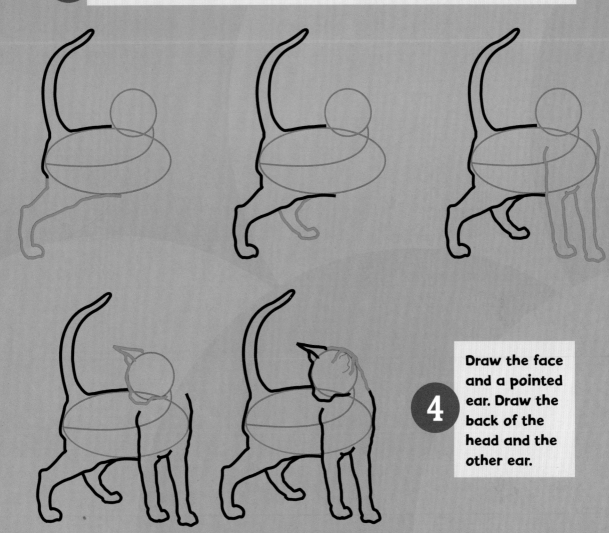

4 Draw the face and a pointed ear. Draw the back of the head and the other ear.

Did you know...

MOTHER CATS TEACH THEIR KITTENS TO HUNT.

5 Carefully erase your center line and base shapes.

ABYSSINIANS
look similar to their wildcat ancestors— or long-ago relatives— who also have lean lines and large eyes.

HELPFUL HINT
Watch cats while they are at play to learn what they look like in motion.

6
Draw an almond-shaped eye. Make a darker circle inside the eye. Draw a teardrop shape for the other eye. Draw an extended triangle for the nose. Add lines for whiskers.

Now it's time to color
your Abyssinian!

A cat
remains still
before it
pounces.

HOW TO DRAW A SIAMESE

Would you like a sly, curious, noisy cat? Siamese cats are a mischievous breed. They meow a lot. They are also considered graceful and aristocratic, or noble. Their long, wedge-shaped faces and sleek, skinny bodies make these cats unique. They also have big, blue eyes. Siamese cats are short-haired. Their coats can be one of four colors: lilac point, blue point, chocolate point, or seal point. Siamese cats can live for more than twenty years.

1 Lightly draw a small base circle and a long center line. Add a long oval. Outline the head shape, and draw two large ears.

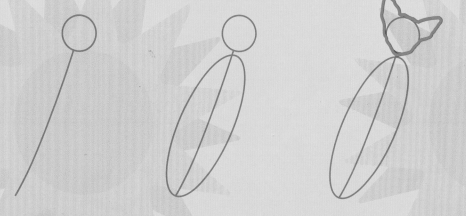

2

Draw a long, slightly bumpy backbone. Add a long, skinny, kinked tail.

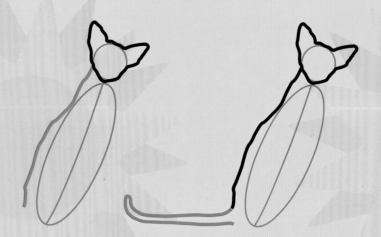

3 Draw the chest and a lifted front leg. Add a short belly line and the other front leg. Finish the belly and back legs.

Fast Fact...

A PAIR OF SIAMESE CATS HAD ROLES IN THE ANIMATED MOVIE LADY AND THE TRAMP.

4 Carefully erase your base shapes and center line.

5

Draw two large eyes. Add a curved line under each. Draw the nose and a small mouth.

FANCY CAT

A cat collar can be stylish. Collars and tags are also helpful. Tags help owners find lost pets.

DRAW A COLLAR WITH TAGS!

A

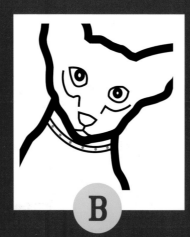

B

C